Old COWDENBEATH

by
Jim Hutcheson

Once a familiar sight on the streets, bakers' carts, such as this one belonging to William Donaldson, delivered their produce to all parts of the town. This particular photograph was taken in Moss-side Road. Along with the goods he had to deliver, the baker also carried a feed bag for his horse, slung at the back of the cart. Cowdenbeath had some of the finest rose gardens in Fife thanks to the efforts of these horses! As the roads got better and the range of goods got wider, the carts got bigger and had four wheels – but as I recall it, all the Co-op carts still had the driver perched on top in all weathers. Some of the other firms used carts with enclosed seats for the driver and they even had room for the customer to get in out of the rain.

© Jim Hutcheson 1998
First published in the United Kingdom, 1998,
by Stenlake Publishing, Ochiltree Sawmill, The Lade,
Ochiltree, Ayrshire, KA18 2NX
Telephone / Fax: 01290 423114

ISBN 1 84033 030 9

THE PUBLISHERS REGRET THAT THEY CANNOT SUPPLY
COPIES OF ANY PICTURES FEATURED IN THIS BOOK.

**I would like to dedicate this book to my uncle, Jimmy Ferguson.
His memory of places and events made my task so much easier.**

INTRODUCTION

Cowdenbeath began as a mere collection of farms and these are remembered today in names such as Thistle Street, Foulford, Moss-side and Cowdenbeath itself. Until the late eighteenth century the area was very poor and the population was gradually drifting away to find work elsewhere. However, when the Oakley Iron Company arrived in 1850 things started to improve. During the process of extracting the iron ore they discovered rich coalfields relatively close to the surface and a series of small pits were established to mine them.

From around 1870 the local mining industry came into its own through a series of improvements such as the introduction of coal cutting machinery in 1884 and, after the formation of the Fife Coal Company in the 1890s, the building of the Central Workshops in the town. The brainchild of the General Works Manager, Charles Reid, most of the equipment used in the coalfields of Fife was manufactured and repaired here and there was also a laboratory for the analysis of coal, dust and air to ensure safer working areas. Surveying, planning and costing departments were all located together, reducing time spent on communications, and the local industry as a whole became much more streamlined and cost effective as a result. (When the mining industry was nationalised in 1947 the Government turned to Charles Reid to help set up the National Coal Board, and much of the organisation was based on his experiences with the Fife Coal Company.)

These improvements in the coal industry led to an increase in local prosperity. Between 1890 and 1910 the population rose from around 3,000 to 14,000, earning the town the moniker 'the Chicago of Fife', and its amenities were transformed. In 1891 a patent apparatus, the first of its kind in Scotland, was installed to provide street lighting from the town's gas works and as the decade progressed there was a series of other improvements such as the building of a new sewage works to help clean up the town (although this later had to be rebuilt because of subsidence). Broad pavements were laid which attracted visitors from all around just for the pleasure of not walking in mud and there was plenty for them to see in the High Street which, according to the local Bailie, was beginning to resemble Princes Street. Free education for miners children was provided in the Public School in Broad Street and an extensive programme of improvements to miners' housing was begun with the building of new estates of houses with running water, inside toilets, bathrooms and electricity.

However, this prosperity was not without cost. Injuries and death were common and the miners had to battle to improve their conditions. Disputes with the coal companies' management became a regular occurrence and lock-outs were to bring back the days of hardship with many families relying on the soup kitchen as their only source of food. This came to a head with the national strike of 1921 when there were running battles between miners and police. This situation culminated with the declaration of martial law in the town when a local pit owner called in the army to deal with riotous miners.

After the 1920s the number of coal fields gradually dwindled and men had to seek work in other industries. But this became increasingly difficult and many left the town in search of jobs. Since then some new industry has arrived but 'the years of the big peys' had gone. I was one of those who left but I still visit frequently. I have many happy boyhood memories of such places as the sawmill at Stevenson's Beath Farm, the Strip Woods, the Cuddy Road, the settling beds at the Water Works, the Moss, Store Treats and Miners' Galas. Do you remember when Woolies had two storeys? Or sledging down the three levels of the school playing grounds? How long is it since there was water in the paddling pool? Whatever your memories, I hope they are of happy times. The town is continually changing and some of the features you know so well today will one day be just a memory, just like some of the pictures in this book. Cowdenbeath may not be the force it once was but it will never be forgotten.

Cowdenbeath's first tram rails were laid in August 1909 in West Broad Street and the six and a half miles to Dunfermline were completed by October. The tram depot at Beath Bleachfield also opened that year. There was initially only one line on the main road, so passing loops were built into the town's network to allow the passage of trams in opposite directions. The tram lines ran all the way from Townhill, through Dunfermline, Crossgates, Cowdenbeath and Lochgelly. There was also a branch line to Kelty which ran from Kelty Junction (closed in 1931). When the network was closed in 1937 the trams were moved to a siding at Hill o' Beath and scrapped.

The construction of the depot. In the picture most of the lines have already been laid and the cobble setts are now being put in place. (The tram lines in Fife were all 3' 6" gauge as the long-term plan was to link major towns throughout the county. This plan was eventually abandoned.) The sub-frames of the trams clearly show the electric motors mounted between the wheels while genuine horse power is still being used by the constructors. The inspection pits have gone now, as have the tram lines and door pillars. The only reminder of the original use of the building is to be seen on both sides of the driveway where sections of tram line take the place of kerb stones.

BROAD STREET, WEST END, COWDENBEATH. 99480.J.V.

The single tram line in this photograph dates it close to 1909 when the line first opened. It was upgraded to double lines soon afterwards, although the life of the tram was ultimately fairly short. The motor charabanc straddling the lines was a sign of the future, although horse-drawn vehicles would still be used for many years. The tram stop on the left would become a bus stop and the tram power lines were eventually adapted to also carry street lighting.

FIFE MINING SCHOOL, BROAD STREET, COWDENBEATH

The origins of this establishment owe much to its first Principal, Dr. Joseph Parker. Opened in 1895, the mining school's first home was in two rooms of Broad Street School until it was transferred to the basement of the new Beath High School in 1910. It finally acquired its own premises on the site of the old Woodside House in 1936. Although it was intended to train apprentices in the mining trade it was also used in 1916 to train women for working in the munitions industry. It was used for this again during the Second World War, although engineering training resumed in 1943. The mining school closed in 1976 and the main building was demolished. The annexe on Moss-side Road is still in use as the Broad Street youth and community centre.

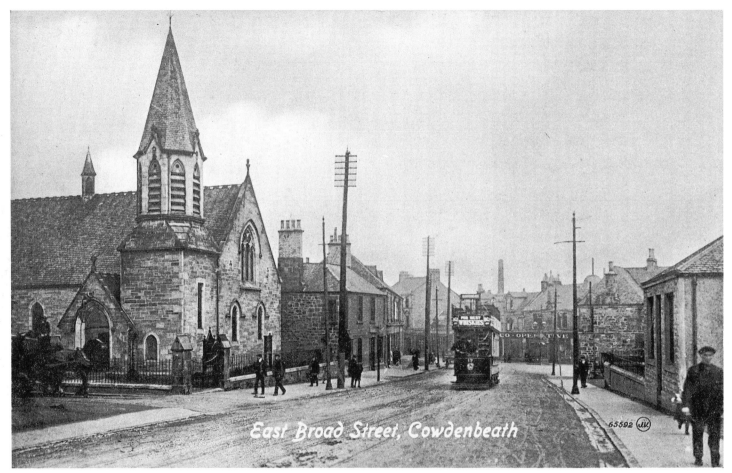

East Broad Street, Cowdenbeath

The West Parish Church was built in 1898 on the corner of East Broad Street and Natal Place to accommodate the growing congregation of the older Beath Kirk. Prior to that a mission had been set up in Brunton's Hall, which can just be seen in the centre of the picture. The new church was called the Chapel of Ease before being constituted as a *quoad sacra* church in 1915 and would remain in use until 1968 when the congregation moved to a new church in Sinclair Drive. At the other end of Natal Place was the Co-op bakery which opened in 1928 and shared the premises with the dairy and stables. For many years it was common to see the horse drawn milk carts emerging from the dairy early in the morning laden with crates of fresh milk to be delivered to nearly every doorstep in the town. On return to the dairy, the milk carts were replaced by bakery carts and the horses and drivers would start again on their rounds.

Although tolls had been collected for some time, it was only after the new road from Queensferry to Perth was built just before 1900 that the toll house became a lucrative source of local revenue. However, by the time this picture was taken around 1920, it had become Jimmy Murray's barber's shop – Jimmy was as well known for his poetry as his skill with scissors and razor. Behind the toll house, across the road, is Brunton's Hall where in 1890 a public meeting confirmed the town's Burgh status and elected the first town council. The following year the council met for the first time and officially selected Cowdenbeath as the town's name. The hall was later acquired by the Co-op and used for a variety of functions, including the annual Christmas Toy Fair which mesmerised wide-eyed children with its display of toys. This building was severely damaged by fire in 1963 and only the valiant efforts of our own part-time firemen, assisted by full time units from Dunfermline, prevented the fire from spreading to other buildings.

High St. Cowdenbeath , B & G.B.

The horses in this *c.*1907 picture still had two more years of peace before clanking trams arrived on the scene. At the far right stands Dick's Co-op building which was built on the site of the original Cowdenbeath Inn. The spire of the Guthrie Church is visible just above the fountain. The Guthrie Church replaced the Free Church, built in Factory Road in 1862 and the first church to be built in Cowdenbeath (the Beath Kirk was actually outside the burgh boundaries). Guthrie Church was demolished in 1974 and the site was renamed Brunton Square.

The Fountain, Cowdenbeath.

The Queen Victoria Diamond Jubilee Memorial Fountain takes centre stage in this photograph dating from around 1915. It was donated to the burgh in 1897 by Henry Mungall who was elected Provost at the first meeting of the new town council in January 1891, a position he held until 1902. The meeting took place in Brunton's Hall which is to the left of the fountain. Of the original nine chosen for the first council another three, James Laing, Andrew Wilson and Charles Barclay, went on to become provosts. The fountain was to remain a focal point until it was removed in the mid-1940s. By that time its ornate cast iron panels and stone base were showing all the effects of the town's smoky atmosphere (one postcard sender wrote 'this is the centre of a mining district and is very dirty'). It then lay abandoned in the council yard in Burgh Road for many years before disappearing forever. The road sign on the left was one erected by the Automobile Association at the request of the town council in 1912.

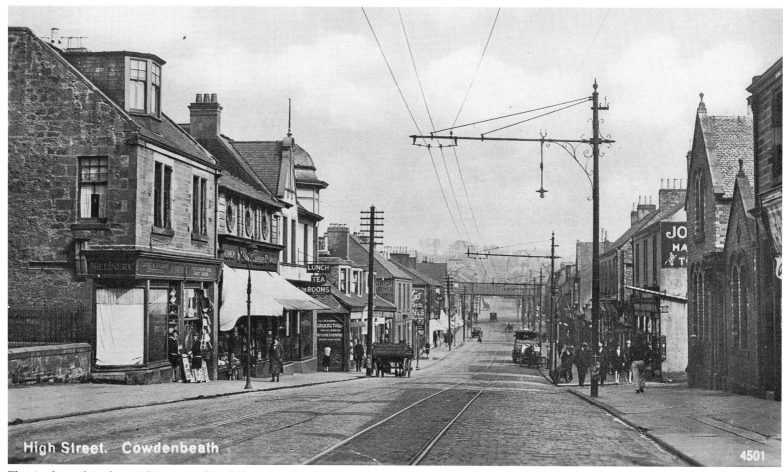

High Street. Cowdenbeath

4501

The single track in the southern part of High Street was later replaced by a double line. Before that there was a passing loop at this spot, which was the terminus for Kelty trams. The town's facilities gradually became more sophisticated, with street lighting supplied from lamp posts rather than from lamps on the tram line stanchion (although in this picture the earlier lamp is still in place). It was not until 1955 that all-night lighting was introduced to High Street, Broad Street and Perth Road, to light the way through the burgh. The horse and cart on the left are outside the D.C.I. tea-rooms, next door to William Low's premises which opened in 1892. Both of these establishments would be taken over by the Co-op in later years. Further along the street was the Burgh Arms which was also used as a meeting place by the town council between 1891 and 1906. Alas, it has gone the way of so many businesses in the High Street, and the building itself has since been replaced.

HIGH STREET, COWDENBEATH.

Wide pavements and a variety of small shops made Cowdenbeath one of the best shopping areas in Fife for many years. The choice today is more limited, but the pavements have been widened further to make even more room for the shopper. On the left, next to the Tea Rooms, lies Paul Place. This leads into the area once occupied by the farm of White Threshes, a strong contender when the name of the town was selected. Nothing remains of this farm or its near neighbour, Cowdenbeath, which was situated to the west of No.7 pit which was just off Pit Road, opposite Bowling Green Street.

RAILWAY BRIDGE AND HIGH STREET, COWDENBEATH. 4486

This picture was taken around the time that the Arcade Picture House burned down in 1954. It stood just out of shot to the right, adjacent to the pedestrian crossing the road. The area through the close just beyond this man was known as 'the back o' Slora's'. John Slora was the owner of the Arcade and the name is still in use! I recall many happy hours sitting in the cafe on the other side of the close in the early sixties. The juke box was the undoubted attraction, even if you couldn't afford to pay for your own selections! Across the road is the butcher shop of Charles Gronbach which opened in 1912 and is still in business. For those who could afford sweets you might be rewarded with a visit to Reeks the dentist which was next door to the Goth which opened in 1895. The Gothenburg system of public houses was of great benefit to the local people as profits over 4% were set aside for the provision of facilities for the community.

COWDENBEATH RAILWAY STATION.

Built in 1900 on the North British line, the new station was designed for passengers only while the old station, behind Dick's Co-op, remained open to cope with the transportation of coal from all the local pits as well as those passengers who were prepared to brave the stour. The new station had a nice warm waiting room, coal fire of course, where passengers could write messages on postcards such as this before posting them in the station's own Post Office. Both of these facilities were on the southbound platform which could be reached by the ornate iron bridge. Young boys would time their crossing of it just as the engine passed below so that they disappeared in clouds of black smoke and white steam. However, it was important not to go home before the smell of the smoke had faded from their clothes – many a warm lug could be attributed to the desire to be an engine driver! The station was modernised in 1961 at a cost of £30,000 but unfortunately lost both its character and facilities in the process.

J.& R. Sharp opened for business on High Street in 1910 and was very popular – the level of success can be measured by the three private lamps on the front of the shop, although I suspect the demand for stays has diminished by now! Further up, on the same side of the road, is the bottom of Stenhouse Street. This came to be known as Duff's Corner after the ironmonger and furniture shop which occupied the site from 1897. It eventually became the Electricity Board showroom. On the opposite corner was Richardson's grocery shop which changed hands to become Young & Arnott's. On the right of the picture is the entrance to the railway station. A steep climb, it paid to make sure you gave yourself plenty of time to catch the train. On the gable end of the building is a sign for P. Williamson, music seller, and if you look at the facade of this building today you will see a plaque with his initials on it.

The previous picture is unusual in that it shows the only stretch of the High Street which didn't have an inn, hotel or bar on it. This section was much more user-friendly to the thirsty miner. Just off picture to the left was The Vaults, latterly Penman's, while the Commercial Hotel and Foulford Arms are on the right. All of these establishments came into being towards the end of the last century. The Commercial is now the Clansman while many years ago the Foulford Arms became Wee Jimmy's. This picture is something of an oddity itself as the tram lines and wires have disappeared from the print. It was probably taken *c.*1919, ten years after the start of the trams (power gantries are visible by the Toon Hoose) and it is certainly before 1925 as the war memorial is not yet in place. Perhaps the puzzled looking policeman on the right is just as baffled as I am!

High Street, Cowdenbeath, looking West.

Contrary to the caption this 1950 picture is actually of the North End of the High Street, with the war memorial visible on the hill in the background. Built in 1925, access to the memorial is by the long climb from the North End or the short climb from Broomfield Road. The trams had definitely gone by the time this picture was taken, but the standards had yet to be removed. Public transport was provided by buses which started out with wooden slatted benches with the upstairs aisle at one side only. The conductors had a bit of a stretch to collect some fares. These soon gave way to the comfort of upholstered double seats with a centre aisle. The shop with the large awning was once the Cowdenbeath Printing Works. Local stationers such as David Clark, John Graham and R. Smith all published their own postcards of the town.

MUNICIPAL BUILDINGS, COWDENBEATH

In 1903 it was decided that new premises were needed for the town council and building of the Municipal Buildings began in 1904. Red sandstone from Dumfriesshire was chosen for the buildings, and as a result the buildings took two years to complete. The opening in 1906 was a grand affair, with schoolchildren given a holiday to watch the proceedings. To further emphasise the importance of the 'Toon Hoose', electric street lights were erected opposite it in 1908. At the time of building, a shed at the side of the site was demolished and this became the entrance into Burgh Road and the council yard. Little has changed over the years. The railings were removed in 1942 as part of the scrap drive for the war effort and twenty years later a new electric clock was installed. The buildings were listed in 1980.

In 1912 the Fife Theatre Construction Company were given permission to erect a new building opposite Foulford Street, designed to seat 1,500 people. An imposing building, the new picture house had no competition after Slora's burnt down. I remember many a Saturday matinee with Hopalong Cassidy or the Cisco Kid putting the West in order. Grown ups got in the balcony, but we kids stayed in the stalls as close to the screen as possible. Although the cinema was granted a licence to operate on Sundays in 1960, it was not enough to save the big screen and the final film was shown two years later. However, the seats were not empty for long as it reopened as a Bingo Hall. Foulford Street was not always linked to the High Street. Access was made by knocking down two buildings.

Through the haze of lum reek several well-known landmarks appear in this photograph. On the left is the town clock and beyond it the chimney of Erskine & Beveridge's Factory. Beyond that is the pit head of No.3 pit, the scene of a mining tragedy in 1895. To the right stands the chimney at No.7 pit, directly behind Foulford School. The long dark building with the arched roof is the Palais de Danse. Formerly the Empire theatre, it was an important place of entertainment in Fife for around fifty years and was also a billet for Polish soldiers during the Second World War. (They also had a camp on the other side of Crossgates where Abercrombie now has its premises.) In the foreground is the Beath Garage which was the first in the burgh to offer servicing for motor cars, and just beyond it is the Crown Hotel which dates from 1887.

PERTH ROAD, COWDENBEATH

Just beyond Miller's shop on Perth Road was the Independent Labour Party Hall. One of those who attended debates there was Jennie Lee who went on in 1929 to become the I.L.P. Member of Parliament for Lanark at the tender age of 29. This was the start of a long and distinguished career in politics which included serving as Minister for the Arts in the Wilson Government. (She also married Aneurin Bevan.) The hall later changed its name to the Haldane Hall and became the property of Cowdenbeath Brass Band in 1952. It was the scene of a disastrous fire in 1968 when not only the hall but many of the band's instruments were damaged or destroyed. However, the hall was repaired for free by the local firm of Harry Street Building Contractors.

PERTH ROAD AND KELTY JUNCTION, COWDENBEATH

This card pre-dates the closure of the Kelty line in October 1931 and shows part of the area which was once known as Morayfield. The Lumphinnans Church was built in 1914 to replace the tin mission hut which had been put up in 1899 on the other side of the railway bridge, to the east of the present church. The church ran very successful Boys' Brigade and Lifeboy groups under the guidance of Alex Scott from Kelty. I well remember loading tents, supplies, possessions and excited participants into the back of Alex' furniture removal van ready for the annual camp which took us to such far flung places as Loch Venacher and Glen Nevis. Great fun was had by all with only the Wednesday visit by our parents to interrupt the week. The church was renamed Cowdenbeath North Church in 1972 when the congregation was merged with that of the Guthrie Memorial Church.

Situated half-way between Cowdenbeath and Kelty, the Netherton Burn was once a very popular spot in the hot summer days of school holidays. Whole families would take the tram, bus or Shank's Pony to have their picnics by the waterside. Sometimes called the Fitty Burn, it flows from Loch Fitty to where it joins the River Ore. There were several small pools in the burn, the most popular of which was the 'dookin hole'. There was plenty to do between paddling, swimming and trying to net sticklebacks. The older boys would sometimes be allowed to follow the burn round to the pond called the Plume where they could swim in deeper water or try to catch some perch. The picnics were often disrupted when the resident sheep or cattle decided to join in the fun – cows are surprisingly fond of corned beef sandwiches!

Foulford School, Cowdenbeath

Foulford School opened in May 1896 with 391 pupils and only four teachers plus the headmaster. With classes of such size it was fortunate for the staff that attendances were poor. The building was very distinctive and was built with bricks produced in the local brickworks at Hill o' Beath. This picture shows the main gates (there was a smaller playground with its own access gate to the rear of the school). An unusual feature was a tunnel under the school linking the two playgrounds and which had a door halfway along it that lead up into the main building. The school's kitchens were to play an important part during the miners' strikes of 1912, 1921 and 1926 when volunteers would supply soup to the families of the town. Two well known personalities connected with the school are the MPs Harry Ewing, who attended as a pupil, and Dennis Canavan who taught there for a short period. The school was demolished in 1976.

STENHOUSE STREET, COWDENBEATH. A.4495

Behind the railings at the bottom of Stenhouse Street is St Bride's Primary School. It was originally the Cowdenbeath RC School and opened in 1904 for the children of the many Irish workers who came to the area as the mining industry expanded. It was renamed in the late 1940s and when it closed in 1973 the pupils were transferred to Moss-side school. The first building on the right is the Roman Catholic church of Our Lady and St Bride which was opened in 1922. Further up the road is the Drill Hall and just above the horse and cart can be seen a light coloured building with a dark door. This was to become the 'tuck shop' so popular with the pupils of Beath High school. On the left is the junction with Pit Road where there was a short row of miners' cottages built very near to the site of the old Cowdenbeath farm.

Drill Hall and Bowling Green Street, Cowdenbeath.

Built for the local company of the Territorial Army, the Drill Hall was opened in 1908. It was the first military building of its kind in Scotland and to mark the occasion it was formally opened by the Secretary of State for War, Mr R.B. Haldane. A very imposing building, it commanded the corner of Bowling Green Street and Stenhouse Street and there was no other building quite like it in town. It was used as the Catholic Institute until St Bride's Chapel was opened, and later became better known as the Tivoli concert hall, as well as serving as a popular dance hall and function room. Boxing matches and public meetings were also held there. As with many other Cowdenbeath buildings, it was demolished to make way for modern housing.

Opened in 1903 in what subsequently became known as Bowling Green Street, this is the older of the town's two bowling greens. The other is behind the Institute in Broad Street. The first president of the club was Archie Hodge who was responsible for sinking the shaft of No. 3 pit and became one of the underground managers. The club went from strength to strength, and the clubhouse was extended by building around the original pagoda-style pavilion. At one time there were also tennis courts where the car park is now. These were constructed in such a way that the courts could be flooded and used as a skating rink in winter. Unfortunately, the base eventually developed cracks and was unable to contain the water needed for the rink. The Brae at the north end of Bowling Green Street was always popular with the youngsters for winter sledging and was equally good for speeding down on home made bogies in summer.

H.G. SCHOOL AND STENHOUSE STREET, COWDENBEATH

Education was an important issue in the lives of hard working miners. Many did not wish their children to follow them down the pits and the best chance of escape was through a good schooling. In 1910 the Higher Grade School was built in Stenhouse Street. This building was similar to the new Town House in both style and the building materials used. However, from the outset there were problems with subsidence as the school was built over the workings of both No.7 and No.8 pits. The rate at which the building sank gave concern throughout its lifetime and various measures had to be adopted to prevent it collapsing. These included shoring up the walls and also running steel rods right through the building. The school has many notable ex-pupils including Jenny Lee, who was Dux; Sir James Black, Nobel Prize winner; and Jim Baxter, who wreaked havoc with England's World Cup Winners in 1967. The writing was always on the wall for this building, along with the cracks, and in 1964 a new high school was built at Kirkford. The old building was eventually demolished in 1990.

Mining has always been a dangerous occupation and it was essential that trained help was able to get to an accident site quickly. This was recognised early on and at the instigation of the Fife and Clackmannan Coal Companies a rescue station was built in Stenhouse Street in 1910, a year before the passing of the Coal Mines Act required such stations to be built. The street was a good site as it was central to the main coal fields of the day. The first of its kind in Scotland, it served 91 collieries and there was no shortage of volunteers. Their record of attendances includes some of the best remembered names in the history of coal mining – Bowhill, Valleyfield, Lindsay and Michael. Within the station there were specially built tunnels and chambers in which the men of the Brigade could practice their skills in comparative safety. There, in darkness, smoke and dust, they trained with the breathing apparatus which was to revolutionise rescue work, and as their expertise was so invaluable they often assisted the other emergency services in rescues away from mining. The station closed in 1987 when operations were transferred to Crossgates.

KIRKFORD COTTAGES & PIT COWDENBEATH.

The pulley wheels and lum of Kirkford pit are in the background of this picture, only about 200 yards from the houses. These were the first miners' raws to be built in the Kirkford area. As with the others of the time, they consisted of two rooms, kitchen and scullery and were owned by the coal company. Water was drawn from a communal tap and everybody would share the outside toilet. For such luxury the occupant was charged 6/- per fortnight. There was no bathroom and the man of the house had to wash himself in a tin bath in front of the fire. One of the myths of the time was that the spine should not be washed as this would weaken the back. Dirty clothes would be washed and hung up in the kitchen to dry in time for the following day. Conditions were such that whole families suffered from bronchial problems. The Coal Companies were reluctant to spend money on improving housing and it fell to the town council to put matters right. This they did with great enthusiasm and by 1919 they had provided 720 new houses, all with proper water and sanitation services, and many more were to follow.

This pit was sunk in 1898 by the Fife Coal Company and produced coal for just over 50 years. Built close to the old North Road at a junction known as Crosskeys it was linked to the other pits in the area by rail and underground. It worked four levels of seams ranging from the highest at 175 fathoms (the Lochgelly Splint) to the lowest at 236 fathoms (the Dunfermline Splint). These seams were twelve feet and four and a half feet thick respectively. Because of the depth of the pit there was a constant battle to keep the workings clear of water and a massive water pump was installed. The stroke of the pump was twelve feet and every stroke could lift 380 gallons of water. Working at its maximum output of four strokes in 60 seconds it could raise six tons of water per minute. The pump was also used to draw water from the pit by local part-time fire fighters on their practice evenings. The fire engine was parked on the flat ground behind the pumping station to the west of the main buildings.

Kirkford Pit. Cowdenbeath.

Women were once expected to work with the men underground but this was stopped in 1842. The women here, standing outside the main winding engine house, would have been employed on the tables at the pithead. It was their job to scan the coal as it passed by on the belts and remove any stones from the load. This could be heavy work depending on the strata underground, but they were so efficient that it was not uncommon for them to sift 1,200 tons of coal a day. The engine house on the right held the steam engines which turned the sixteen foot drum holding the cables which supported the cages. As the two cables were wound on in opposite directions, one cage would descend and the other rise as the drum turned. This was all controlled from the pithead by a series of bell signals. Two sets of pulley wheels can be seen here. One set was used for coal only while the other carried men or coal. Winding speeds were faster when only coal was in the cage and the maximum two ton load could be raised from the 236 fathom mark in just 40 seconds.

Kirkford Village, Cowdenbeath

JV 72939

Sited on the old Great North Road this rural scene disappeared in the first half of this century. The opening of a new north road through the centre of Cowdenbeath, combined with the arrival of motor transport, meant there was no longer any need for the village smiddy, and the stables and blacksmith shop fell into disrepair and eventually closed. However, the road continued to be used by the people of the burgh as it leads to the Kirk o' Beath and adjoining cemetery – the cemetery lodge can be seen at the bend of the road beyond the trees.

There has been a church on this site since at least 1170 and the present Beath Church remains the burgh's oldest building. The church had served all the farms in the area for centuries but by the sixteenth century it had fallen into ruins. However, its popularity was restored in 1640 when it was rebuilt. It has an association with the infamous Burke and Hare who made several visits to the graveyard and grave-robbing became such a problem that methods of preventing the removal of bodies were introduced such as putting metal boxes over the coffins and laying very heavy flat stones over the grave. These were left in place until the body was of no use to the robber and were so heavy that lifting gear was needed to shift them. By 1884 the church was too small for the growing congregation of miners and an extension was added. In 1897 the post of gravedigger became vacant and there were 50 applications for the position – it would seem that a miner could use his shovel anywhere!

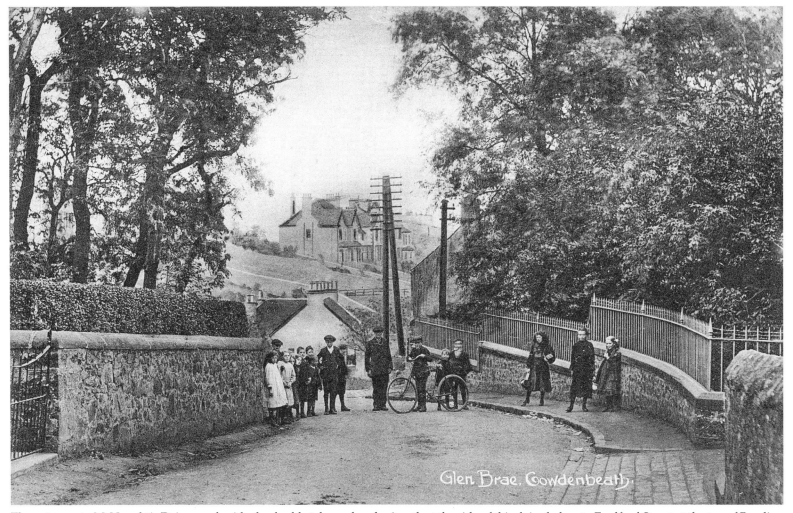

Glen Brae, Cowdenbeath.

The entrance to McNaught's Dairy was beside the double telegraph pole. A path at the side of this dairy led on to Foulford Street at the top of Bowling Green Street and is still in use. The large houses up on Bervie Hill were the homes of the merchants and managers of the day. Accessed from Perth Road or the North End via Broomfield Road, they had a commanding view over most of the town – or they would have had if the smoke haze wasn't too thick. These houses have been joined by others now but the cottage on the Brae has gone.

Foulford Road, Cowdenbeath

72940

A view further down the Brae. Judging by the unshod feet it is likely that these children are from the miners' raws, not the houses on Broomfield Road. Just visible to the right of the road is the roof of the Glen Tavern which has been in existence since the early 1900s. Some years ago a club was formed in the tavern with a strong nostalgic background. To qualify for entry, members had to ca' their gird up and down the Brae, an easy task on today's smooth road surface. There was a different technique in ca'ing a gird with a stick or one of the deluxe models with cleek attached. Many a bairn would take his gird when sent to the shop rather than walk along without it!

THE GLEN, FOALFORD ROAD, COWDENBEATH 1687

Just behind the pillar on the right was a spring which in early times supplied water to the inhabitants of this end of the town. Latterly it became one of the best places in the area to collect frog-spawn and tadpoles. Known as Cressy Burn, the water flowed eastwards under the road and alongside the garage and Haldane Hall at the North End. The driveway on the right still leads into the Public Park but nearly all the houses in this picture have been demolished and replaced by modern buildings.

Foulford St, Cowdenbeath, B & G.B.

Running parallel to Foulford Road, this street had miners raws on both sides. They all had to share a communal water supply and outside dry toilets. These raws were small communities within the town. The neighbours would all pull together in times of hardship – and there were plenty of these. At the far end of the street stood the Communist Hall which provided entertainments for children as well as a meeting place for the adults. Communism had a strong hold in the area and the local branch was organised by Bob Selkirk who later became a member of the town council.

ENTRANCE TO THE PUBLIC PARK, COWDENBEATH. 4493

The Public Park was laid out in 1910 and opened in 1911, the cost being met by donations from the Public House Society which gave over £7,000 to the project. There was one main roadway through the park which gave access to the swing park, paddling pool, football park and band stand. The park was also the venue for the 'Store Treat' which was held every year. Parties of well scrubbed bairns met at the various branches of 'the Store' (the Co-op) and marched behind brass or pipe bands to assemble in Broad Street School playground. From there the whole procession made its way along the High Street to the park where games and sports were the order of the day, interspersed with music from the bands. Every child was given a poke which contained a cake, fruit and sweets.

40

This ornate bandstand was the venue for many Sunday afternoon concerts. Set in the middle of the valley, it was the focal point of the Public Park with paths radiating out from it. Although benches and chairs were provided it would seem that the grass was more comfortable. The concerts were very popular and the local brass band performed here on many occasions. The S.C.W.S. band played to large audiences in 1933. Earlier, in 1926, the bandstand was put to another use when the miners' leader A.J. Cook addressed a rally of 20,000. It was put to the same use in 1984 when one of the largest strike rallies in Scotland was addressed by Mick McGahey, the Scottish miners' leader. The bandstand has been removed and an octagonal flower bed marks the spot where it stood.

This spot is actually nearer to Burntisland than Cowdenbeath. Situated to the south of the Cullaloe Cuts the cottage no longer exists but if you look closely at the roadside you can still make out the wall and gate. The registration number of the car seems to be prefixed FG, which would signify that it was registered in Fife. Further along the road, on the way back to Cowdenbeath, you can also see the ramparts of a bridge. This is called the Queen Mary's Brig and is a double bridge of the same style as that in Dunfermline's Pittencrieff Park with two arches, one on top of the other.

The mines almost exclusively employed men, but women could find work in shops, in service, or in the factory. Erskine and Beveridge's linen factory opened in Cowdenbeath in 1890. It produced high quality damask linen and in its heyday had 500 looms working. These were arranged in the conventional way of four in a square. One weaver was responsible for all four looms and her wage was based on her output. Linen was a good material to work with as smashes and broken wefts were not as common as with the silks used, for example, in Winterthurs factory in Dunfermline. The machinery was driven by belts from central shafts and the noise in the main factory was incredible, making speech almost impossible. The heavy and dirty work of maintaining and servicing looms was carried out by the tenters. As the demand for man-made fibres grew, the linen industry shrank and the factory was closed in favour of the main premises in Dunfermline.

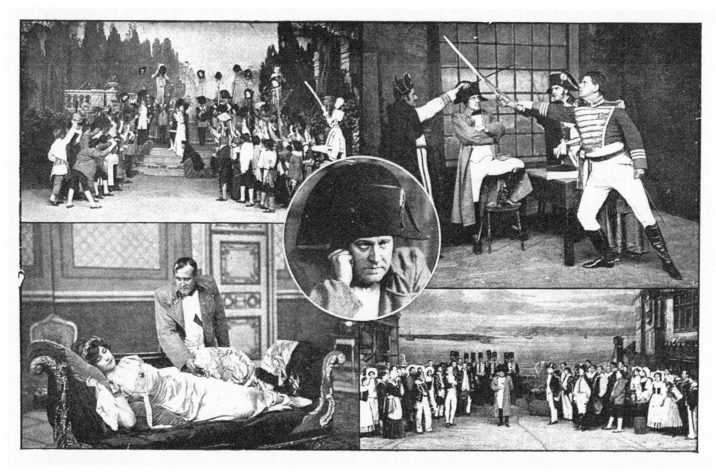

A promotional card for the Empire Theatre advertising the coming attraction of 'A Royal Divorce, a Story of Waterloo', starring Eve More and George Hudson. Owned by Geordie Penman, the Empire attracted many of the top names of the time including Will Fyfe, Charlie Chaplin and Harry Lauder. It was also used as a roller skating rink and a dance hall. Later, the name was changed to the Palais de Danse and attracted acts such as Acker Bilk, Johnny Dankworth and Joe Loss, who called it the best provincial ballroom in the country. Pop performers such as The Honeycombs and Gene Vincent also came. The latter appeared in 1961 and such was his popularity that a police escort had to be provided. Perhaps the cost of bringing such megastars to town was too high for the Palais as it had to shut its doors in the mid-sixties. It was taken over by an English light textile firm and opened as a factory in 1966. The prominent black vaulted roof finally disappeared in smoke and flames six years later.

This team of shopkeepers and assistants usually played on their half day, hence the Wednesday title. They competed in the Half Day Holiday League and were very successful in the 1911-12 season. They played at North End Park which they presumably shared with the 'big' team who played there from 1888 until 1914. Football was very popular and there were originally two teams carrying the name of Cowdenbeath: Rangers and Thistle. These two amalgamated and took the name Cowdenbeath Rangers in 1881, dropping the Rangers tag the following year. (Another Cowdenbeath team was called Raith Rovers – does anybody know what happened to them?) Apparently, the club had financial problems right from the start and the players actually paid the club to get a game.

These two members of Cowdenbeath Pipe Band are of particular importance to me. The Bass Drummer was my father, Geordie Hutcheson, and the Piper my uncle, Jimmy Ferguson. When they joined the band in the thirties it had already been in existence since the turn of the century. The band used to practice in the old winding house situated behind Woolies but had to move to premises close to Sharp's Outfitters in the High Street. Then, when the Haldane Hall became available they moved there and shared it with the Brass Band. In 1953 it won the Grade 3 world championship held at Stirling and by the late sixties it had gained promotion to Grade One and attained fourth place at the Cowal Games. The band broke up for a number of years but has since restarted. Unfortunately, all the uniforms and instruments have disappeared in the meantime. If you know of their whereabouts I am sure the band would love to hear from you.

A pug engine parked at the Central Workshops prior to being broken up. Most of the engines that puffed their way between the pits of Cowdenbeath met the same fate. The pug was a powerful 0-4-0 engine which, for its size, had huge pulling power. This is possibly an engine called the *Fordell* which was transferred from the Fordell Colliery Company along with the *Alice* and *Lord Hobart* engines. The *Lord Hobart* was the largest of these engines, weighing 33 tons fully laden, and differed in that the boiler extended forward of the saddle tank. All of these engines were designed to operate on the Fordell Railway which had rails with a 4' 4" gauge and had to be altered to work on the main lines which measured 4' 8½". They were also designed to travel under low bridges so the cabin roof was lower than normal.

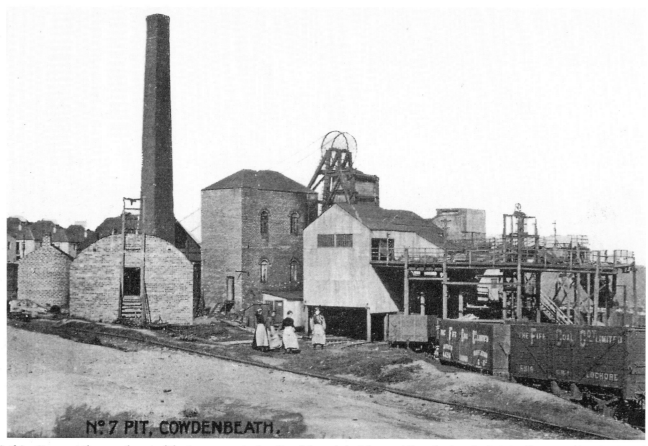

No. 7 PIT, COWDENBEATH.

Sunk in 1860, this pit was at the very heart of the town near to the site of the original farm of Cowdenbeath. Originally owned by the Cowdenbeath Coal Company, it was sold to the Fife Coal Company in 1896 along with five other pits, including Mossbeath, at a cost of £227,500. No.7 was a single shaft pit and was connected to Mossbeath in the late 1930s to give better ventilation. Even so, the fans had to work hard to keep fresh air in the pit. The intake was right next to Pit Road and irresistible to any youngster with a spare sheet of paper to plaster against the wire mesh! The shaft was also connected to Kirkford Pit via the Dunfermline Splint, a distance of 1,400 yards – water in No.7 was pumped along this underground road to Kirkford where it was pumped up to the surface. No.7 was also connected to the other pits and the workshops by rail. The tracks crossed the High Street at the side of Slora's and the opening is still known as the level crossing. The pit employed 570 men at the height of production but this had fallen to 372 men by the time the coal seams were exhausted. The last working pit in Cowdenbeath, my own grandfather, James Ferguson, was killed here in 1948. It was shut in 1960 and with it closed a chapter of history.